WHY DO BRUISES CHANGE COLOR?

✦ and other questions about blood ✦

Angela Royston

Heinemann Library
Chicago, Illinois

Designed by Joanna Sapwell and StoryBooks
Illustrations by Nick Hawken
Originated by Ambassador Litho
Printed by South China Printers, Hong Kong

07 06 05 04 03
10 9 8 7 6 5 4 3 2

Library of Congress Cataloging-in-Publication Data
Royston, Angela.
  Why do bruises change color? : and other questions about blood /
Angela Royston.
      p. cm. -- (Body matters)
Includes index.
Summary: Answers common questions about blood and the circulatory
system.
  ISBN 1-40340-202-7 (HC)   ISBN 1-40340-457-7 (PB)
  1. Blood--Juvenile literature. 2. Cardiovascular system--Juvenile
literature. [1. Blood. 2. Circulatory system.] I. Title. II. Series.
  QP91 .R855 2002
  612.1'1--dc21
                        2002003543

Acknowledgments
The author and publishers are grateful to the following for permission to reproduce copyright material:
pp. 4, 5, 9, 12, 13, 26 Science Photo Library; pp. 11, 16, 17, 18, 23, 27, 28 Gareth Boden; p. 14 Getty Images;
p. 22 Trip; p. 24 David Walker; p. 25 Powerstock.

Cover photograph by Gareth Boden.

Every effort has been made to contact copyright holders of any material reproduced in this book.
Any omissions will be rectified in subsequent printings if notice is given to the publisher.

Some words are shown in bold, **like this.** You can find out what they mean by looking in the glossary.

CONTENTS

WHY DO CUTS BLEED?

If you fall and cut yourself, red blood oozes out of the wound. It does not matter where the skin is broken, it always bleeds. This is because your skin is crisscrossed by tiny tubes that carry blood. The tubes are so narrow you can see them only under a microscope. But you can see the blood that leaks out when some of them are damaged.

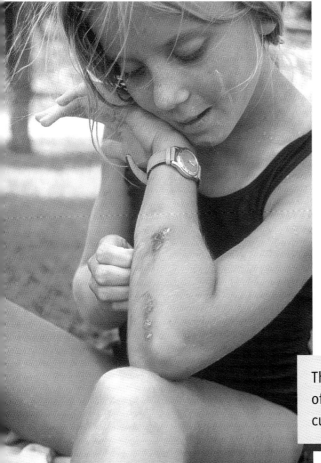

This girl has fallen off her bicycle and cut her arm.

Keeping dirt out

It is important not to let dirt and germs get into your body through the wound. Bleeding washes dirt and germs out of the cut and helps to protect the body. Make sure a cut is clean and cover it with a bandage. Rubbing a little antiseptic cream on the inside of the bandage also helps to kill germs.

Is bleeding dangerous?

It might look frightening to see blood trickling from a cut, but do not worry. Older children have about 1 gallon (4 liters) of blood, so your body will not miss a little bit. If the cut is very deep and blood is pouring out, then it is important to get help fast to stop the bleeding.

DO NOT TOUCH SOMEONE ELSE'S BLOOD

Blood can carry germs, so it is important not to let other people's blood inside your body. Always use a paper towel or a clean cloth to clean someone else's cut.

This photograph has been magnified so that you can see the tiny tubes that carry blood through the skin.

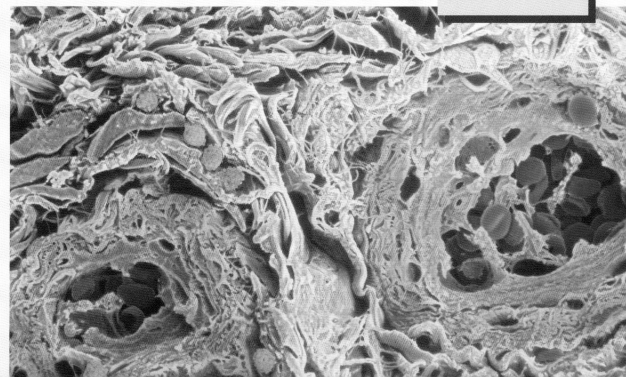

Capillaries

The tiny tubes that carry blood through your skin are called **capillaries.** There are capillaries in every part of your body, including your bones and muscles and all the **organs,** such as your liver, heart, stomach, and brain. Only your hair and nails are not filled with blood. There is blood under your nails but not in the nails themselves. This is why they do not bleed when you cut them.

Arteries

Capillaries are part of a one-way system of tubes that carries blood from the heart around the body and back to the heart. The heart pushes blood into large tubes called **arteries.** One artery goes from the heart to the lungs. The largest artery is almost 1 inch (2.5 centimeters) wide. It takes blood from the heart to the rest of the body. It branches into narrower arteries: one for each arm, two to your head, and one to your lower body. Each artery branches into narrower and narrower arteries and then into capillaries.

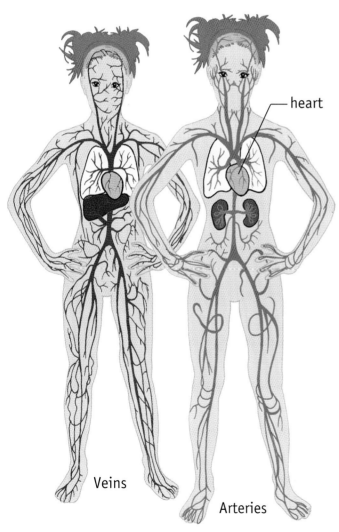

heart

Veins

Arteries

Veins

When the blood has reached the farthest capillaries, it begins to travel back to the heart. The capillaries join together into wider tubes that lead into the **veins.** You can see some of the veins that carry blood back to your heart on the inside of the wrist. The veins join up and take the blood into the heart.

A NETWORK OF TUBES

Tubes that carry blood are called **blood vessels** and you have about 60,000 miles (96,000 kilometers) of them. Most are capillaries. If all your blood vessels were laid out end to end, they would stretch around the world twice.

Capillaries link the arteries to the veins. Blood travels through the capillaries in each part of the body and then into the veins.

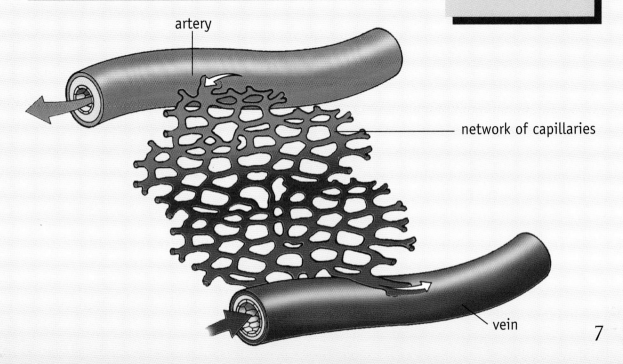

artery

network of capillaries

vein

7

WHY DO CUTS FORM SCABS?

Scabs are the body's way of protecting an open wound while the skin below it heals. When the skin is damaged and broken, it bleeds. As blood flows through the wound, it becomes thicker and starts to clot.

Sticky blood cells

Blood contains special **cells** called **platelets.** They stick together to form a plug in the walls of the damaged **capillaries.** Other chemicals in the blood form a web of strands across the wound. Platelets become trapped in the web and form a large clot of blood mixed with other cells. This dries to form a hard scab that keeps out dirt and germs.

When you damage your skin, the wound heals by forming a scab.

How a wound heals

1. A clot of blood forms over the wound and stops the bleeding.

2. The clot hardens and shrinks to form a scab.

3. New skin grows below the scab.

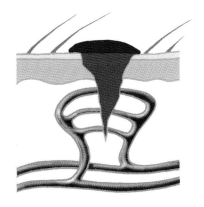
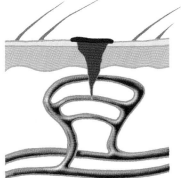
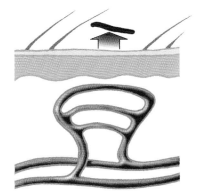

New skin

The body is very good at repairing itself. The walls of the capillaries that were torn or cut are soon replaced. New skin slowly grows across the wound. At the same time, the scab dries out and begins to shrink. When it falls off you can see the new, pink skin underneath. Do not pick a scab before it is ready to fall off. If you do, the wound below may open up and start to bleed again.

Large wounds

A large wound or deep cut may have to be stitched to help it heal. Only a nurse or doctor should do this. The stitches hold the edges of the wound together while it heals. Wounds that are stitched do not form scabs, but they may leave a scar. Scars slowly fade, but can last for years.

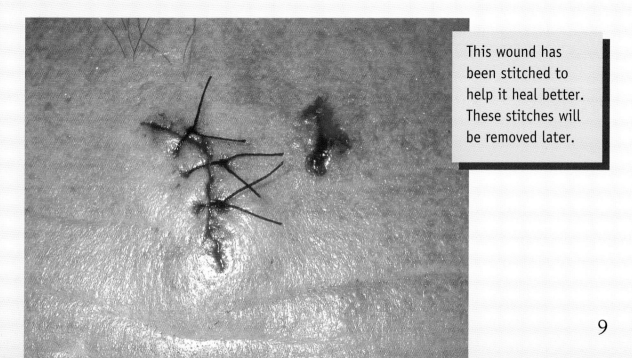

This wound has been stitched to help it heal better. These stitches will be removed later.

WHY DO BRUISES CHANGE COLOR?

A bruise is caused by bleeding below the skin. The blood below the skin slowly breaks down and is absorbed by fresh blood. As this happens, the bruise changes color from blue-black to purple to yellow.

What causes a bruise?

Underneath your skin are layers of fat and muscle covering your bones and **organs** such as your stomach and liver. If something sharp hits the skin, it cuts through it and you bleed. But if something blunt hits the skin, the force of the blow is spread out over a large area. The skin is not broken but some of the tiny **capillaries** in the skin and flesh below may be damaged. Blood leaks from the capillaries into the flesh around them.

This boy fell downstairs and has a large bruise on his shin. The bruise is blue-black to begin with, but it changes to yellow as it slowly disappears.

bruise

Swelling

When any part of the body is damaged, extra blood floods into the area. The blood helps to repair the damage. The extra blood makes the skin look red and can make the flesh swell. The swelling forms a cushion around the damaged area and protects it from further damage. If you fall and knock your head, for example, a lump might quickly form on your scalp or forehead.

How a bruise heals

When the **cells** of the spilled blood die, they turn blue-black. It can take a few hours for a bruise to show below the skin. But it takes many days for fresh blood to destroy and remove all the dead cells.

This girl is holding an ice pack over a bump on her head. The cold helps to reduce the swelling and to make the bump less painful.

WHY IS BLOOD RED?

Blood contains three main types of cells—red cells, white cells, and platelets.

Blood is made of a watery liquid called **plasma** with billions of tiny blood **cells** floating in it. The three main types of blood cells are red cells, white cells, and **platelets.** Blood is red because it has more red cells than any other type of cell.

Red cells

The red substance in red blood cells is called **hemoglobin.** The main job of red blood cells is to carry oxygen from your lungs to all the cells in your body. The oxygen sticks to the hemoglobin and turns it bright red. When the hemoglobin lets go of its oxygen, it becomes dull red.

White cells and platelets

White blood cells kill germs that get inside your body and also remove dead cells. White cells are larger than other blood cells. They surround the germ or

Platelets

Plasma

White blood cells

Red blood cells

dead cell and destroy it. Platelets are small cells that help your blood clot when you cut yourself.

Short life

Each red blood cell lives only for about four months, so your body has to constantly make new cells to replace the dying ones. It makes about two million new red blood cells every second. New red blood cells are made in the **marrow,** the soft, spongy substance in the middle of some bones. Some white cells, however, can live for many years.

MILLIONS OF RED CELLS

A drop of blood no bigger than the head of a pin contains 9,000 white cells, 250,000 platelets, and 5,000,000 red cells. An adult has about 1 ⅓ gallons (5 liters) of blood. This means the adult has about 25 billion red cells.

Blood cells are too small to see except through a microscope. This woman is looking at a sample of blood to find out whether it is healthy.

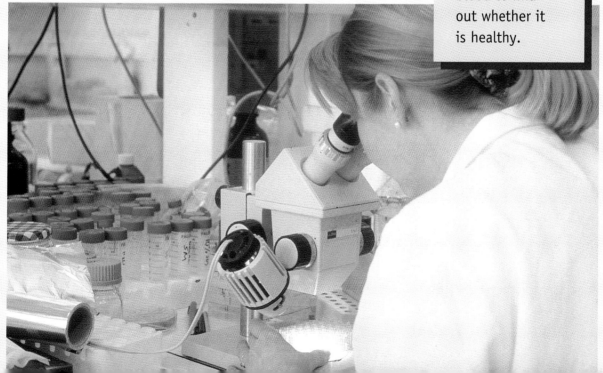

Many kinds of cells

Every part of the body is made up of tiny **cells.** Your skin is made of skin cells, your bones of bone cells, and so on. Every living cell needs food and oxygen to keep it alive.

A transportation system

Blood is a kind of transportation system. It delivers food and oxygen to every cell and takes away waste. The food you eat is broken down in your stomach and **intestines,** and the useful parts pass into the blood. It is taken to your liver and stored. The liver keeps your blood stocked with a good supply of glucose, the substance your cells burn to get the energy they need to do their job.

You need to eat food to stay alive. When the food has been processed by the digestive system, it is carried in the blood to every part of the body.

Taking away waste

As a cell uses glucose it produces heat and the gas carbon dioxide. This waste gas is carried in the blood back to the lungs. Here it leaves the blood and joins the air that you breathe out.

Other things carried in the blood

The blood carries many things apart from food and oxygen around the body. If you take a pill to cure a headache, for example, the chemicals in the pill are carried around your body in your blood. When they reach your head, they help it stop the ache. Alcohol and other poisons pass into the blood too. The liver destroys poisons but it can only deal with small amounts at a time. Alcohol in the blood affects many parts of the body, including the brain.

The blood supplies each cell with food and oxygen. It carries away carbon dioxide.

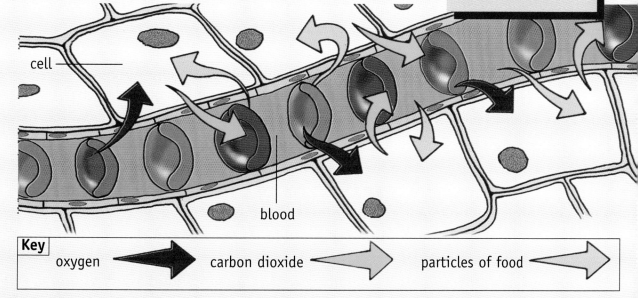

cell

blood

Key | oxygen ➤ | carbon dioxide ➤ | particles of food ➤

WHY DO MY FEET GET COLD FIRST?

The body makes most of its own heat by burning food. The temperature of most of your body is normally 98.6° Fahrenheit. Blood carries heat from the center of the body to your hands and feet, but it loses some of its heat on the way. Since blood has to travel farthest to reach your feet and toes, they are usually the first to become cold. Your fingers may also feel cold, because blood has to travel a long way to reach them too.

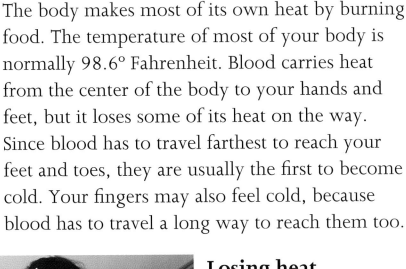

Wear warm socks and slippers to help keep your feet warm.

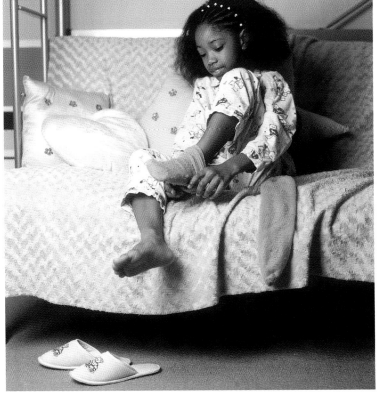

Losing heat

Most heat is lost from your body through the tiny **capillaries** in your skin. When you are in a cold place, the capillaries become narrower. This means that less blood comes to the surface of your body, so less heat is lost. But it also means that your toes and fingers get less warm blood and feel even colder!

Stamping your feet and rubbing your hands makes them warmer. It brings more warm blood into your fingers and toes.

Warming up

When you are cold, a good way to warm up is to move around and exercise your muscles. Muscles make heat as they work. The blood takes in this heat and carries it around your body. The harder you exercise, the faster your heart beats. This pushes the warm blood around your body faster.

Cooling down

Blood also helps to cool you down when you are hot. The capillaries in your skin become wider. This makes your skin red and hot but it allows some of the heat to escape from the body.

WHAT DOES MY HEART DO?

Your heart is more or less in the center of your chest between your lungs and behind your breastbone. If you place your hand here, you will feel your heart beating.

The heart pumps blood to the lungs and around the body. First, blood leaves the heart and goes to the lungs. Here it takes in oxygen before returning to the heart. The heart then pumps blood that is rich with oxygen around the body.

What does my heart look like?

Your heart does not look very romantic. It is a slimy, throbbing **organ** that fills and spurts with blood. The heart is made of a special kind of muscle that is very strong. Muscles work by contracting, which means getting smaller. When the heart contracts, it squeezes blood into the **arteries.** The force it produces is about the same amount of force it takes you to squeeze a tennis ball.

How big is my heart?

Curl your fingers into the palm of

your hand to make a fist. This is how big your heart is. The bigger you are, the bigger your heart is, but the bigger your fist is too. An adult's heart is also about the same size as their fist.

Circulation

Blood circulates around the body, but each drop of blood does not go to every part of the body. Instead the arteries, **capillaries,** and **veins** form several separate systems. For example, some blood goes to the head and back to the heart. A large artery takes blood to the lower body but it branches into several main arteries. Each of these arteries has its own circulation system.

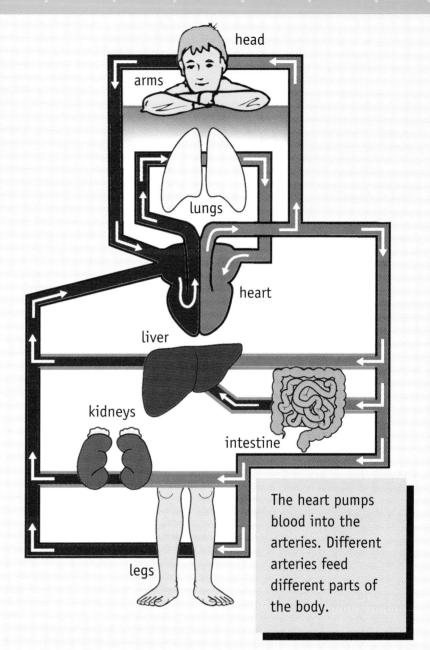

head

arms

lungs

heart

liver

kidneys

intestine

legs

The heart pumps blood into the arteries. Different arteries feed different parts of the body.

CONSTANT CIRCULATION

Blood travels around the body almost 2,000 times a day. So every drop of blood passes through the heart about once a minute.

19

Inside the heart

A heart is divided into two halves. Each half has two spaces, or chambers. This is because the heart is not one pump, but two pumps that work together. The chambers on the right side pump blood to the lungs. Those on the left side pump blood to the body. The left side is slightly larger than the right because it has a bigger job to do.

Journey through the heart

Blood from the body is brought into the upper right chamber and flows into the larger, lower chamber. As the heart contracts, the blood is pushed through the **artery** to the lungs. There it picks up oxygen and returns to the left side of the heart. It flows from the upper into the lower left chamber. From there it is squeezed into the artery that takes it to the body.

TIRELESS HEART

The heart never rests. It usually beats at least 60 to 70 times a minute. So it beats:

- about 4,000 times every hour
- nearly 100,000 times a day
- over 2,500,000,000 times in an average lifetime.

Valves

The heart has four **valves** that control the flow of blood and make it flow only in the right direction. Valves between the upper and lower chambers open to allow blood to flow into the lower chambers. They close as the heart contracts. At the same time valves between the lower chambers and the arteries open. Now the only way the blood can go is out of the heart and into the arteries.

veins from body

vein from lungs

valves closed

valves open

right side of heart

left side of heart

artery to lungs

artery to body

valve closed

valve closed

valves open

Valves between the upper and lower chambers open to allow blood from the **veins** to flow in.

As the heart contracts, the valves from the upper chambers close and those to the arteries open, forcing the blood through them.

WHAT KEEPS MY HEART BEATING?

A group of **cells** in the right, upper chamber controls your heart-beat. These cells are the heart's **pacemaker.** They produce a wave of electrical signals that spreads through the heart muscle and makes it contract.

ECG

Doctors use a machine called an electrocardiograph (ECG) to check on whether a patient's heart is beating properly. **Electrodes** are placed on the patient's chest. They pick up the heart's electrical signals. The machine either displays the signals on a screen, or it prints them out.

The ECG machine records the electrical signals that make the heart beat. They show up as blips on the screen.

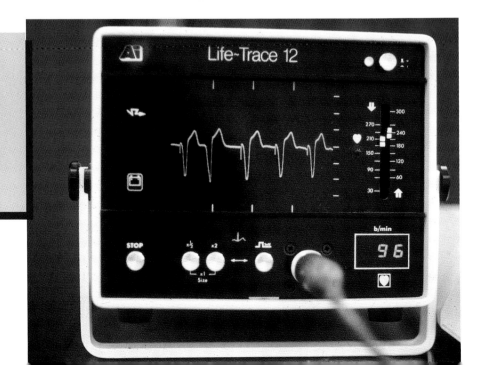

Measuring your heartbeat

You can measure your own heartbeat by taking your **pulse.** If you place your fingers over your wrist as shown below, you will feel a regular throb. Every time the heart beats it causes a wave of blood to spurt through the **arteries.** It is the spurt of blood that you feel as a pulse.

Stethoscope

Doctors use a stethoscope to listen to your heartbeat. It magnifies the sound so that they can hear your heart working. What they hear sounds like "lub-dup." It is the sound of the **valves** slamming shut. The "lub" sound is made when the valves between the upper and lower chambers close. The "dup" sound is made when the valves to the arteries close.

ARTIFICIAL PACEMAKER

Sometimes the heart's pacemaker stops working properly. Then doctors fit an artificial pacemaker just below the skin. It is powered by batteries and sends a regular signal to the heart to tell it to beat.

This boy is measuring his own pulse. He counts how many beats he can feel in a minute.

WHAT MAKES MY HEART BEAT FASTER?

Many things can make your heart beat faster, including exercise, fear, and some drugs.

Exercise

Muscles take oxygen and food from the blood to give them the energy they need to work. When you exercise, your muscles work hard and use more oxygen and food. You gulp in extra air and your heart beats faster to supply the muscles with oxygen and food. Exercise strengthens all of your muscles and makes them work better. This includes the muscles in your heart.

Running makes your heart work faster and better, so that it supplies your muscles and brain with extra oxygen.

Fear

If you feel scared or anxious, your heart may beat faster. If a snarling dog suddenly jumps at you, your heart may begin to pound. Your body speeds up your heartbeat and sends extra blood to your brain and muscles. You become more alert and your muscles tense, ready for action.

Drugs

Caffeine in tea, coffee, and soda is a drug that makes your heart beat faster. You probably will not notice your heart beating fast, but you will feel more alert. Some drugs make the heart beat dangerously fast. For example, using inhalants can cause a heart attack.

This woman is parachuting for the first time. Her heart is probably beating very fast!

FAST DELIVERY

Normally your heart pumps about 1 ⅓ gallons (5 liters) of blood a minute around the body. When you exercise, your heart can pump 7 gallons (25 liters) of blood a minute.

WHAT CAUSES A HEART ATTACK?

A heart attack occurs when part of the heart muscle stops working. The heart has its own **arteries** that supply it with blood. If one of these arteries becomes blocked, the muscle does not get enough oxygen and stops working.

Blocked arteries

A person suffers from heart disease when the arteries that supply the heart fill up and become narrower. The heart has to work harder to push blood through them. Heart disease can cause pain, so the problem is often diagnosed before a heart attack occurs. A surgeon can sometimes unblock the arteries and make them wider again. If this operation does not work, the patient may have a heart bypass operation, in which the damaged arteries are replaced with healthy **blood vessels.**

A surgeon is pushing a narrow instrument through the arteries of the patient's heart. It will unblock the arteries to make the heart healthier.

A healthy life

Heart disease is one of the most common causes of death among people who are over the age of 50. The best way to avoid heart disease when you are older is to live a healthy life when you are young. There are four main ways to keep your heart healthy: do not smoke tobacco, avoid fatty foods, exercise regularly, and stay calm.

Smoking

Smoking tobacco affects the heart in several ways. Carbon monoxide in tobacco smoke takes the place of oxygen in the blood, so that the body, including the heart, is deprived of oxygen. Nicotine in tobacco makes the arteries constrict and become narrower. When people smoke regularly, their hearts and their arteries are permanently damaged.

A person who smokes is twice as likely to have a heart attack as a nonsmoker.

Fat and cholesterol

Many fatty foods contain a substance called cholesterol. Cholesterol sticks to the inside of the **arteries** and makes them narrower. People with high cholesterol, people who are overweight, and people with a lot of stress are more likely to suffer from heart disease. The best ways to cut down on cholesterol and lose extra fat are to eat healthy food and exercise.

Exercise

Regular exercise will make your heart work better so that it pumps more blood through your body with every beat and does not have to work so hard. You should exercise so that your heartbeat is increased for 20 to 30 minutes at least three times a week.

Stress

Stress makes your heart beat faster. If this happens for long periods of time, your heart may become strained.

These are some foods that are good for your heart.

BODY MAP

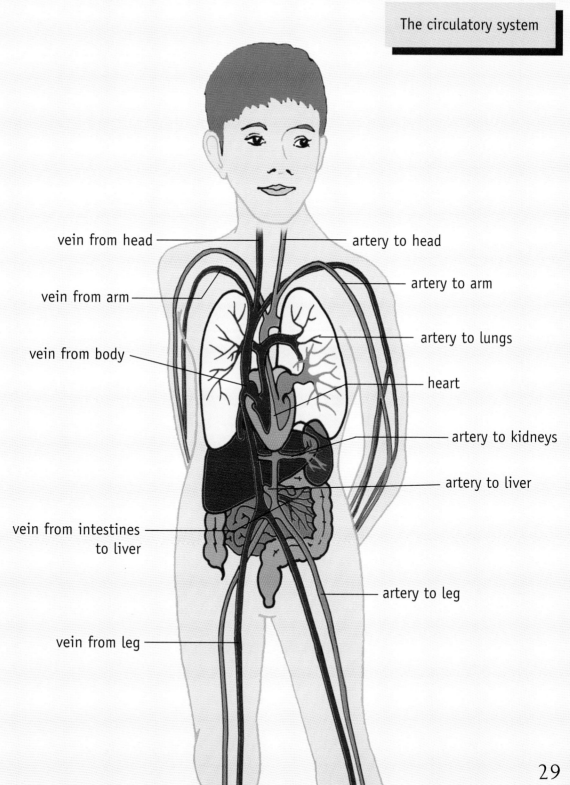

vein from head — ——— artery to head

——— artery to arm

vein from arm —

——— artery to lungs

vein from body —

——— heart

——— artery to kidneys

——— artery to liver

vein from intestines
to liver —

vein from leg —

——— artery to leg

29

GLOSSARY

artery   blood vessel that carries blood from the heart to other parts of the body

blood vessel   tube that carries blood

capillary   very thin blood vessel that joins the ends of the arteries to the veins

cell   smallest building block of living things. The body has many kinds of cells, including different kinds of blood cells, bone cells, and skin cells.

electrode   device that conducts electricity

hemoglobin   red substance in red blood cells that joins with oxygen from the lungs and carries it to all the cells in the body

intestine   long tube that food passes into after it leaves the stomach

marrow   soft, spongy substance found at the center of many bones

organ   part of the body, for example the heart, that carries out a particular process

pacemaker   group of cells in the heart or an artificial device that sends out signals to make the heart beat regularly

plasma   clear liquid that other kinds of blood cells float in

platelet   kind of blood cell that helps to heal wounds by making blood clot

pulse   throb or beat that can be felt at various points of the body. It is caused by a surge of blood as the heart contracts and is used to measure heartbeat.

valve   device that controls the flow of a liquid or gas. Valves in the heart open and close to allow blood to flow through the heart. Valves also prevent blood from flowing in the wrong direction.

vein   blood vessel that carries blood from the capillaries back to the heart

FURTHER READING

Hardie, Jackie. *Blood and Circulation*. Chicago: Heinemann Library,1997.

Parramon, Merce. *How Our Blood Circulates*. Broomall, Penn.: Chelsea House, 1994.

Stille, Darlene. *The Circulatory System*. Danbury, Conn.: Children's Press, 1997.

INDEX

$24.22

DATE			

JAN - 2004